MASTERFUL
Machine Pieced Quilts

Jean Biddick

American Quilter's Society
P. O. Box 3290 • Paducah, KY 42002-3290
www.AmericanQuilter.com

Located in Paducah, Kentucky, the American Quilter's Society (AQS) is dedicated to promoting the accomplishments of today's quilters. Through its publications and events, AQS strives to honor today's quiltmakers and their work and to inspire future creativity and innovation in quiltmaking.

EXECUTIVE BOOK EDITOR: ANDI MILAM REYNOLDS
SENIOR BOOK EDITOR: LINDA BAXTER LASCO
GRAPHIC DESIGN: ELAINE WILSON
COVER DESIGN: MICHAEL BUCKINGHAM
QUILT PHOTOGRAPHY: CHARLES R. LYNCH
HOW-TO PHOTOGRAPHY: JEAN BIDDICK

Additional copies of this book may be ordered from the American Quilter's Society, PO Box 3290, Paducah, KY 42002-3290, or online at www.AmericanQuilter.com.

Text © 2010, Author, Jean Biddick
Artwork © 2010, American Quilter's Society

Library of Congress Cataloging-in-Publication Data

Biddick, Jean.
   Masterful machine-pieced quilts / by Jean Biddick.
      p. cm.
   ISBN 978-1-57432-659-8
   1. Machine quilting--Patterns. 2. Patchwork--Patterns.
I. Title.
   TT835.B48152 2010
   746.46'041--dc22

                                        2009049227

COVER AND RIGHT: LOOKING HIGH & LOW, details. Full quilt on page 82.

Acknowledgments

Thanks to:

Pam Ashbaugh
Suzanne Bishop
Jo Cady-Bull
Carol Carpenter
Janet Downing
Jessica Duke
Kathleen Nitzsche
Christine Porter
Judy Sheridan
Kathryn Wald
Sally Gould Wright

For sharing their quilts.

Kathleen McCulloch

For making a new sample of ALISON'S QUILT and testing the pattern.

Alison D'Bue

For taking photographs of the Truro Cathedral floors.

My students

For allowing me to nudge, prod, and encourage them to piece quilts that they think are beyond their capabilities.

Linda Lasco

For her gentle guidance through the editing process and for her friendship.

Elaine Wilson

For her incredible computer skills that turned my sketches and drawings into polished diagrams.

Charles R. Lynch

For his extraordinary quilt photography.

My family

For their encouragement, patience, and love.

Contents

7 Introduction

10 Tools & Supplies

14 Basic Techniques: TRURO STAR

20 The Details

30 About the Projects

   32 ACCIDENTAL STARS

   36 SIMPLY CIRCLES

   40 ALISON'S QUILT

   46 NEW DIRECTIONS

   52 CAMPANILE

   58 ABEER'S GIFT

   68 PESWARA

   74 TRESSA

   81 LOOKING HIGH & LOW

90 Gallery

95 About the Author

GEMSTONE, detail, 16½" x 16½", made by the author. Christine Porter challenged several quilters to use some of the designs from her quilt VENETIAN INSPIRATIONS to create their own designs. I used a miniature version of part of her central motif and surrounded it with two of the other designs. GEMSTONE is machine pieced and machine quilted. This quilt is not patterned.

Truro Mosaic II, 88" x 88", made by the author. This design comes from
the central crossing of Truro Cathedral in Cornwall. I recreated the design as closely as I could from photos taken at the cathedral. After making
Alison's Quilt and testing the freezer-paper piecing method I felt confident
that I could tackle this large project. The quilting is done by hand with a
variegated over-dyed pearl cotton in a random pattern that is reminiscent of
the veining found in marble. This quilt is not patterned.

Introduction

My introduction to tile floors as a design source for quilts was a lecture by Christine Porter, well-known in both England and the United States as a teacher, quilt show judge, and author. After showing us examples of floors in Bristol Cathedral in Bristol, England, she mentioned several other English buildings with interesting floors. One of those was Truro Cathedral in Cornwall. At the time my husband and I were in the planning stages for a trip to Cornwall and had started making lists of places we wanted to see. Truro Cathedral immediately moved from the if-we-get-time list to the must-see list. During our visit to the cathedral other people were looking at carvings, windows, and statues while I was captivated by the wonderful geometric patterns in the floors.

Geometric mosaic designs are an established art form in many cultures, but the mosaics that first captured my attention are of a style called Cosmati design. Their development is attributed to a family of Italian stonemasons who thrived from about 1100–1300 A.D. A very famous Cosmati pavement can be seen at Westminster Abbey in London. The Great Pavement of Westminster Abbey was laid by Italian craftsmen in 1268 for Henry III. The floors of Truro Cathedral are much more recent. The cathedral was built between 1880 and 1910, but the floors echo the designs from the Italian pavements of those earlier centuries (fig. 1).

FIG. 1. The geometric designs on the floor around the baptistry of Truro Cathedral include many traditional quilt patterns.
PHOTOS: ALISON D'BUE

MEDICI MEETS THE DRAGONS, detail, 47" x 47", made by Christine Porter, Bristol, England
PHOTO: J. NEIL PORTER

The interlocking bands of pieced triangles and squares create wonderful patterns, but traditional piecing methods are not particularly helpful in translating the designs into quilts. The designs are intricate, but I was sure I would be able to find a way to make the piecing work. After all, if Italian stonemasons could cut unyielding stone and arrange the pieces in these beautiful patterns there was no reason I could not do the same with fabric that bends and flexes enough to give me some wiggle room.

Of course, later it occurred to me that those stonemasons had one advantage that I did not have—grout. Wouldn't it be wonderful if someone invented quilter's grout that would fill up any irregularities when our piecing isn't quite as accurate as we hoped it would be?

FIG. 2. The triangles are cut with the ¼" seam allowance added. It is difficult to see how they should be sewn together. Should the pieces match at the left edge or the right edge or somewhere in between?

When I started working on a quilt based on the floors of Truro Cathedral I knew I would need to use more than basic piecing techniques. The shapes, while often basic triangles, do not always contain nice comfortable 45-degree angles. In addition, there are seldom repeated pieces that are exactly the same size and shape as each other. The patterns would need to be constructed one piece at a time. I would not be able to cut 296 half-square triangles that would all finish to 1½". And once the seam allowance is added to the odd angled pieces it would be difficult to see exactly how the edges should be aligned for piecing (fig. 2, page 8).

If I were hand piecing, the seam line would be drawn on each piece and I would be able to tell exactly how to align the pieces for sewing, but this didn't seem to be the best choice for machine piecing. I knew many quiltmakers were using freezer paper for appliqué work and that several were starting to use freezer paper for pieced work as well. I decided to experiment to see if this was a reasonable choice for my mosaic designs (fig. 3).

The basic idea of freezer-paper piecing is that you start with a full-sized drawing of your pattern. It is a flat piece of paper. Once you cut the freezer paper apart and use it for templates, you sew along the edges of the paper. After the puzzle of flat pieces of paper is put back together, the attached fabric becomes a flat quilt.

There is never only one way to do things. This freezer-paper template method can be handled in several different ways and you are encouraged to adapt the instructions to fit your own particular needs. This is certainly not a speed piecing method. It is detailed and exacting, but is a good choice for projects that do not fit nicely into the standard square and half-square triangle designs that account for so many pieced quilts.

Fig. 3. With the freezer-paper templates in place it will be easy to match the corners of the papers and align the triangles perfectly.

Tools & Supplies

Making Patterns

There are several tools that will make it easier for you to draw or trace the full-size designs that are needed for a mosaic quilt.

Tracing vellum or butcher paper
Freezer paper
Yardstick compass (also called Compass
 Points)
Protractor
Colored pencils
Graph paper
Removable tape
Ping-Pong® table
Tweezers

PATTERN PAPER

You will need to find wide paper for drawing your master pattern. Tracing vellum is a good choice but it can be difficult to find and is often expensive. Another choice is white butcher paper. You can often find this in a store that caters to elementary school teachers. Both these products come in rolls that are 30"–36" wide. That is wide enough for many projects and two or more widths can be taped together for larger projects. Some people use the paper that is meant for a doctor's examination table. I find that this paper is too thin and tears too easily.

FREEZER PAPER

Freezer paper can usually be found in your grocery store. It comes in both 12" and 18" widths. It is easier to work with the wider roll of paper since you will often need to tape together several pieces to cover your master pattern.

YARDSTICK COMPASS

Many tile designs include circles or partial circles. Since you are drawing a full-size pattern, you will need to draw circles that are beyond the capability of a standard compass. A yardstick compass consists of two small metal pieces that slide onto a yardstick and can be adjusted the proper distance apart so you can draw circles that are very large. One piece has a pencil lead and the other a sharp point for the center of your circle. The compass can also be put onto a 1" x 12" Plexiglas rotary ruler. This will allow you to draw circles up to about 22" across, but is less unwieldy than a longer yardstick. You can also cut a yardstick in half. This gives you a long enough compass to draw a circle nearly 35" in diameter (fig. 1, page 11).

PROTRACTOR

When drafting your own circular designs, you will need to divide the circles into an even number of pieces. A protractor will make this job easier. Of course, you will need to remember how to use it!

COLORED PENCILS

This is a hint offered by one of my students. When working with circles it is necessary to add registration marks that will make it possible to align the circles after each ring has been constructed. They need to go back together in the same alignment as they were when the drawing was made. If you draw two or three different colored lines across your freezer-paper pattern it will be easy to see where the rings align for a perfect fit (fig. 2).

GRAPH PAPER

When you are drafting your own mosaic pattern, it is often helpful to start with a small version before tackling the full-size drawing. Graph paper with a ¼" grid can be helpful as you figure out how the various pieces fit together. The graph paper drawing will also make it easier to enlarge the design as you make your full-size drawing.

REMOVABLE TAPE

When you are tracing your full-size pattern onto the freezer paper, you do not want the two papers to move. Taping them together will allow you to make your copy without having to continually realign the drawings. Removing the freezer paper from your master pattern after you have made the copy can be difficult and the paper can get torn. The answer is removable tape, which can be removed without tear-

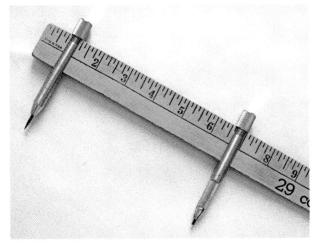

FIG. 1. Yardstick compass

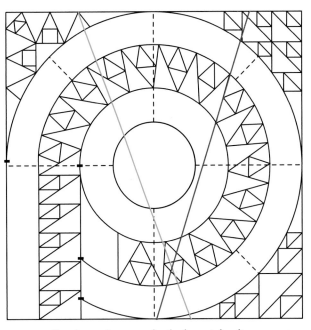

FIG. 2. Registration marks help with alignment.

ing the paper. The tape comes on a roll like regular cellophane tape, but is labeled "removable tape" and can be found in office supply stores and sometimes in larger drug stores.

PING-PONG TABLE

If you are doing a very large drawing, it is helpful to have a very large table. The best drawing surface I have found for this purpose is a Ping-Pong table.

Construction Supplies

There are also several items that will make the construction of your tile design easier.

Well-maintained sewing machine
Open-toe presser foot
Single-hole throat plate
Thread
Needles
Iron
Tweezers

SEWING MACHINE

Keep your sewing machine cleaned and oiled. It will be happier and so will you. Use the standard stitch length of about 2–2.5 (10–12 stitches per inch on older machines). In traditional paper piecing you need to sew with a very small stitch to make removing the paper easier. This is not necessary with the freezer-paper template method as you are sewing next to instead of through the paper.

OPEN-TOE PRESSER FOOT

Find a presser foot that gives you a good view of the needle area of your machine. You want a foot that is open all the way to the front so you can see what is arriving at the needle and can watch as the needle skims the edge of the freezer paper.

SINGLE-HOLE THROAT PLATE

The throat plate on a zigzag machine has a wide opening to accommodate the needle as it swings from side to side. This opening is not conducive to good straight stitching. Replacing the plate with a single-hole throat plate will improve your piecing. It will give you a straighter line of stitching and will help keep the needle from pushing the fabric down into the hole. Do remember to change back to the regular throat plate before doing any zigzag sewing!

THREAD

A good quality thread is important. A 50-weight cotton thread is my preference for most of my piecing. For miniature quilts I like to use a 60-weight cotton thread as it is thinner and takes up less room in the seam. In either case, I recommend a good quality, recognized brand name thread. Cheaper threads are made with shorter fibers and can be very linty. You will spend all your time cleaning your machine instead of sewing. Choose a thread that blends nicely with your fabrics. You may find it necessary to use more than one thread color for your project. Usually using one thread that is the color of your lightest fabric and one that is the color of your darkest fabric will be sufficient.

NEEDLES

Use a Sharp needle instead of a Universal needle. It will pierce the fabric more easily and give you a straighter line of stitching. Match the needle size to the thread you are using. A #70 or #80 Sharp is a good match for a 50-weight cotton thread. A #60 or #70 Sharp is a good match for a 60-weight cotton thread.

IRON

I prefer to use a steam iron set on the cotton setting. If you have trouble getting the freezer paper to stick to the fabric you might try using a dry iron instead. You might also experiment with the temperature setting to find the combination that works best for you. You may find that the freezer paper adheres better to fabric that has been washed. Washing out the chemicals and sizing used in the manufacturing process may make it easier for the paper to stick to the fabric.

TWEEZERS

Even though you do not sew through the freezer paper it can be difficult to remove some of the papers. A pair of tweezers can be used to help reach papers inside the narrow points that are difficult to reach with your fingers.

ABEER'S GIFT, detail. Full quilt on page 59.

Basic Techniques: Truro Star

Fig. 1. The star found on the chancel steps of Truro Cathedral. PHOTO: ALISON D'BUE

Fig. 2. Our project star, simplified from the star in Truro Cathedral

The best way to understand the basics of my freezer-paper piecing technique is to make a small project. The Truro Star pattern we will use is a simplified version of a motif found on the chancel steps of Truro Cathedral (fig. 1).

This star is so easy to draft that I am surprised it does not form the basis of any traditional star patterns that I have been able to find (fig. 2).

Step 1. Make a master pattern. This will be a full-size drawing of the design.

Note: For a fairly simple drawing like this, you may find it faster to draft your design directly onto the dull side of the freezer paper.

For our star sample, start by drawing a square. This can be any size. Something between 9 and 15 inches is a good choice. Locate the center of each side and make a dot.

Connect the dot at the center of each side to the two opposite corners of the square (fig. 3, page 15).

Step 2. Cover the design with freezer paper. If you need to join two pieces of paper, be sure to tape along the entire edge of the butted seam. Do not use regular transparent tape. It will melt

 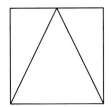 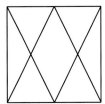 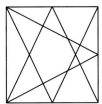 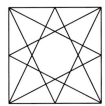

FIG. 3. Draft the star one step at a time.

when ironed. Use masking tape or blue painter's tape instead. Use removable tape to secure the freezer paper to the master design with the dull-side up. You do not want the freezer paper to move while you are making your copy. Trace the master design onto the freezer paper.

Step 3. Label your freezer-paper copy.

Each pattern piece needs a number, a grain-line mark, and a fabric choice.

NUMBERING: The numbers can be assigned in any order that makes sense to you. Keeping all the numbers in the same orientation (right-side up so you can always locate the top of the drawing OR around a circle so the top of the number is always at the outside edge of the circle, etc.) will make reassembly easier.

Note: With some patterns, the master drawing may be numbered before the freezer-paper copy, in which case, number your pattern to match.

GRAIN LINE: Make a decision about where you want the grain line of each piece. On the outside edge of your design you want the straight of grain to run along the finished edge

of the star. Bias edges on the outer edge of a square wouldn't make any sense. On the star points you might want the grain line to run from tip to base.

FABRIC CHOICE: Your labels can be specific (the red fabric with the blue feathers) or general (dark, light, warm, cool, background) (fig. 4).

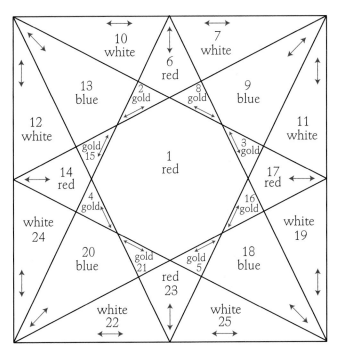

FIG. 4. The freezer-paper copy has been labeled. Each piece includes a number, a grain-line indication, and a fabric choice.

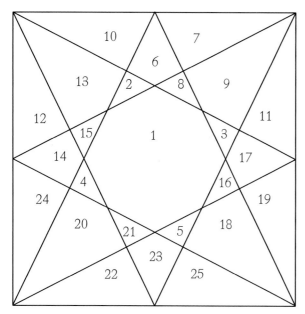

FIG. 5. The master drawing is labeled and each piece has the same number as the freezer-paper copy.

FIG. 6. The freezer-paper pattern is being cut apart. The pieces are sorted according to the fabrics from which they will be cut.

FIG. 7. The freezer-paper templates have been ironed to the appropriate fabrics. Space has been left between the pieces to allow for seam allowances. The grain-line indications have been used to properly orient the paper pieces on the fabrics.

Step 4. Number the pieces in your master drawing. You will need the numbered master drawing to help in reassembling your design. Use the same numbers you used on the freezer-paper pattern. The master drawing may or may not include the grain lines and fabric choices (fig. 5).

Note: *If you drafted your design directly onto freezer paper you do not have a master drawing. In this case make a small sketch of the design and number it to match your freezer-paper pattern.*

Step 5. Cut the freezer-paper pattern apart. Use a rotary cutter. Start with the longest straight line you can find. Cut the pattern apart until each numbered section is a separate piece of paper. As you cut, sort the pieces into groups based on the indicated fabric choice (fig. 6).

Step 6. Iron the freezer-paper pieces onto the wrong side of the appropriate fabrics. A steam iron works well and takes very little time to adhere the pieces to the fabric. Be sure to leave at least ½" between the pieces so you will have room to add a ¼" seam allowance to each piece (fig. 7).

Step 7. Cut out the pieces. Use a rotary ruler with an easily identified marking ¼" from the edge. Align the ¼" mark with the edge of the freezer paper and cut the fabric. This adds the seam allowance to each edge of the pattern piece (fig. 8).

Step 8. Lay out the pieces using your numbered master drawing as a guide (fig. 9).

Step 9. Separate the pieces into sections that can be easily pieced. Look for places where there can be a long straight line. Separate the pieces along that line. Continue moving the pieces until you can see a pattern of sections for piecing (fig. 10).

FIG. 8. The ¼" seam allowance is added as the fabrics are cut.

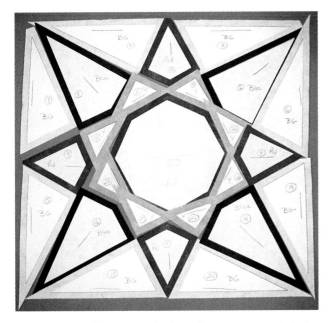

FIG. 9. The fabrics with their freezer-paper labels are arranged with the help of the master drawing.

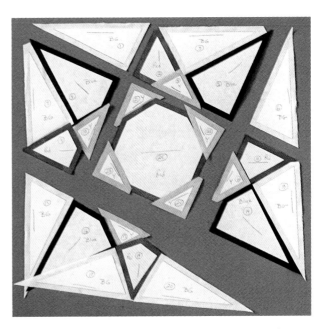

FIG. 10. The pieces of the star are separated into sections.

Fig. 11. The triangles have been pinned to the center octagon. The needle of the sewing machine should just graze the edge of the paper as you sew next to it.

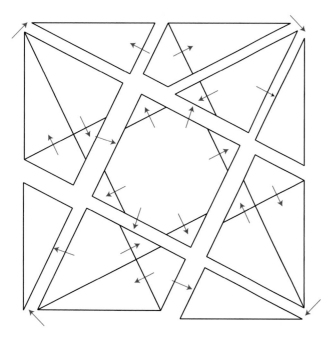

Fig. 12. Press seams as shown by the arrows.

Step 10. Add the corners to the center octagon. Place a pin through the fabric at the corner of the triangle and then through the fabric at the corresponding corner of the octagon. These pins are positioning pins that assure proper placement of the triangles. Without the freezer paper as a guide it would be difficult to see how these pieces need to fit together. The pins are now dangling through the two layers of fabric and you cannot sew this way. Use additional pins to anchor the pieces as aligned, then remove the positioning pins. (See pages 22–23 for detailed pinning instructions.)

Sew next to the freezer paper with your normal stitch length. Your needle should just graze the edge of the paper but not sew through it. Press the seams toward the triangles (fig. 11).

Step 11. Continue piecing each of the sections you identified in Step 9. Press the seams as indicated (fig. 12).

After you have sewn several pieces together you will have intersections that need to be pinned. Place a pin through the fabric at the corner of the paper and at the seam line of the intersection. Then place that pin through fabric at the seam line and corner of the paper of the underneath section. This is again the positioning pin. Be sure that the pin is pulled all the way to the pin head so the layers of fabric that need to match are actually touching each other. Place anchoring pins through the fabric and paper about ⅛" to the right and to the left of the positioning pin. Remove the positioning pin before sewing the seam.

▶▶▶▶▶▶▶▶▶▶▶▶▶▶▶▶▶▶▶▶

Step 12. Remove the freezer paper only after all the edges of a piece have been sewn (fig. 13).

FIG. 13. The partially completed Star block seen from the back

FIG. 14. The completed Star block

The Details

CORNISH NIGHT, 23" x 23". Made by the author. This quilt is not patterned.

FIG. 1. The drawing for a non-symmetric quilt is the reverse of the finished quilt.

Drawing & Preparation Details

If your design is not completely symmetrical you will need to draw your pattern as a reversed image of the way you want it to look when it is finished. The freezer paper will end up being a complete drawing on the back of your pieced top. When you turn the top over the image will be reversed (fig. 1).

Number the drawing in any way that makes sense to you. These numbers do not represent the sewing order. They are only used as a road map so you can put the pieces back together after they have been cut apart and ironed to the back of the appropriate fabrics. What is important is that the numbers on your master drawing and the numbers on your freezer-paper pattern match. You will use the numbers on the master drawing as you lay out the ironed and trimmed pieces. The master drawing will help you put every piece back in its proper position.

I like to use tone-on-tone, batik, and hand-dyed fabrics. Busy prints may get lost in these detailed designs. Solid fabrics will highlight any piecing irregularities. Tone-on-tone and batik fabrics add subtle interest to the designs and can help camouflage any small piecing problems that would be blatantly obvious with solid fabrics. Batik fabrics add color variations that would be difficult to achieve if you tried to find that many actual different fabrics. You get the diversity and added interest without the added effort.

As you cut apart the freezer-paper pattern, sort the pieces into piles based on the fabric choice for each piece. For some patterns the piles will be "background" and "everything else." For others you will have one pile for each color family. For still other patterns you may have piles for specific fabric designs like the "green leaf" and "blue plaid."

Sorting the pieces as you cut them apart is much more efficient than cutting all the pieces of the pattern and then going back to sort them. For the largest patterns you may want to cut only one section at a time and iron those pieces onto their fabrics before cutting the rest of the pattern.

Many patterns use a variety of fabrics for each color choice or a random scattering of many colors against a black background. It actually takes a bit of effort to make your fabric choices look random. Here is what works for me.

If my pattern calls for many black fabrics, I first cut apart the freezer-paper pattern and make a pile of all those pieces that are supposed to go on the black fabrics. Then I re-sort the pieces by number, making a pile of all the 20s, all the 30s, and so on. If I have 100 pieces, I will have 10 piles of paper pieces.

Then I check to see how many pieces there are in total and how many fabrics I have available. If there are 10 fabrics I will need to put 10 pattern pieces on each fabric. I will take one piece from each pile and put them with a fabric. Then I will take a second piece from each pile and put them with a second fabric. I will continue this process until I have 10 pieces of paper with each of the 10 fabrics.

If I have the same 100 paper pieces but am using 20 fabrics, I will only need to put 5 paper pieces with each fabric. I can take a paper piece from every other pile so that I have the 5 papers for each fabric. This system will help spread the different fabrics out over the entire design.

When ironing the papers to the back of the fabric I use a steam iron on the cotton setting. It takes very little time for the shiny part of the freezer paper to melt and adhere to the fabric. You may need to experiment with different iron settings to see what works best for you. I know some quilters who use only a dry iron and some who swear by a cool iron. Try changing the settings to see if one particular combination seems to work best for you.

Occasionally I have had a pattern piece that does not want to stay on the fabric or there'll be a piece with a long point that will continually lift off the fabric. I first try to re-iron the paper and hope it will decide to behave. If that does not work I may lightly mark the outline of the paper on the fabric so I will still have the seam line as a guide even if the paper is missing by the time I am ready to sew that piece. You do *not* want to resort to gluing the paper onto the fabric. It will be difficult or impossible to remove the paper later.

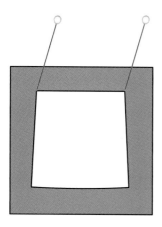

Fig. 2. Place positioning pins at the corners of the freezer paper to align the pieces.

Fig. 3. Pin across the seam line to anchor the pieces for sewing and remove the positioning pins.

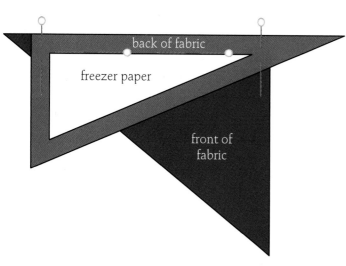

back of fabric

freezer paper

front of fabric

Fig. 4. On longer seams, parallel pins along the edge of the freezer paper will help ensure that the back layer does not shift while you are sewing.

Piecing Details

Careful pinning will result in more accurate piecing. To join two pieces, start by placing a positioning pin through the top layer of fabric exactly at the point of the paper piece. Then put that same pin into the fabric piece underneath, again exactly at the corner of the paper (fig. 2).

Pull the pin tight so the two fabrics are touching each other. Hold the fabrics in place so they will not move, remove the pin, and pin again at a flat angle across the corner. If you leave the pin in place and just turn it to pin it through the corner you will push the bottom layer of fabric out of position. Holding the fabric tight after it is aligned, removing the pin, and replacing it at a shallow angle instead of in a stabbing manner will keep the points matched more accurately. Pin the other end of the seam in the same manner (fig. 3).

If the seam is short (about 1½" or less) the pins at the two ends of the seam will be enough to hold everything in place as you sew. If the seam is longer you will need to add an additional pin or pins along the seam line to keep the edges matched properly. These extra pins are placed in the seam allowance along the edge of the freezer paper instead of perpendicular like the end pins (fig. 4).

After placing a pin, check underneath to be sure the pin lies accurately along the freezer paper in the back as well as in the front. You will not be able to see this match while you are sewing so be sure it is properly pinned before you begin to sew. You will be able to sew over the perpendicular pins at the ends of the seams, but will need to remove the parallel pins as you come to them.

After you have several pieces together you will begin pinning seams that include previously sewn intersections. You will need to pin at these intersecting seams to create accurate matches and perfect points. If the seams were pressed to one side you will be able to see the corner of the freezer paper and place the pin at that point. If the seams were pressed open you will need to fold back the seam allowance to find the corner of the freezer paper. In either case use a positioning pin stabbed straight down to match the intersection. Pull the pin tight so the fabrics touch each other and add an anchoring pin to each side of the seam to hold the match in place. The positioning pin can then be removed. The anchoring pins should be perpendicular to the eventual seam line, going in through the seam allowance and out below the seam line through the paper (fig. 5).

When possible sew with a previously pieced section on top and a plain piece on the bottom. Being able to see the previous stitching can help you see intersections and points. It also helps avoid the problem of seam allowances underneath getting flipped and caught improperly in the seam. You will be able to see these seam allowances and keep them flat. If you are sewing a curved seam you will not always be able to have the pieced section on top since you will need to have the concave part on top at all times.

After sewing each seam, trim the tails of any fabric that extend past the seam allowance. If a bit of fabric extends after pressing a section,

trim that excess as well. Keeping tails trimmed and edges neat will reduce bulk and make it easier to do accurate piecing on the next step.

Handling Specific Motifs

There are several shapes and units that occur in more than one pattern. Details of sewing each of them are presented here and not repeated for each project.

Partial seam: A partial seam is used when there is not a complete dividing line across a section, but the intersecting lines are still at right angles. There is not a Y-seam involved. Sew part of a seam to create a long edge for another piece to fit against. Add pieces around the edge until you can return to the original seam and sew the rest of it closed (fig. 6, page 24).

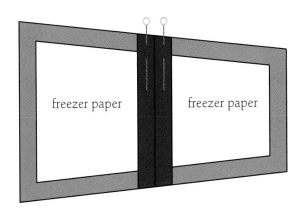

FIG. 5. When pinning an intersection, use one positioning pin to align the corners of the freezer paper, then two anchoring pins to hold the match in place.

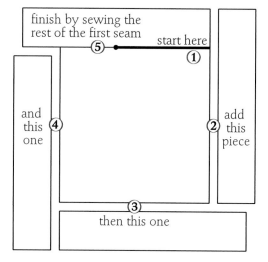

Fig. 6. Example of a partial seam

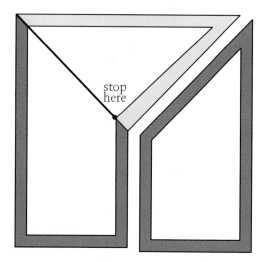

Fig. 7. Example of a Y-seam

Y-seam: You need a Y-seam when three seams meet in a single point and you cannot sew all the way from one outside edge to the other in a straight line. Sew one of the seams, stop without sewing into the seam allowance, and backstitch. Some sewing machines want to take an extra stitch as you change from forward to reverse sewing. This can make it difficult, but not impossible, to stop at an exact point. Pay attention to how your machine handles back-stitching so you can stop exactly where you want to. Sew the second seam and backstitch at exactly the same point as before. Sew the final seam backstitching again without sewing into the seam allowance (fig. 7).

Checkerboard: A double row of squares (or nearly squares in the case of a curved piecing section) makes up a checkerboard. Be sure to mark the grain line at the inner edges of the squares and be consistent. Join the squares in pairs, matching grain lines as shown. Press the seams toward the darker fabric. This will allow for abutting seam allowances when you join the wedges to each other. As you join the wedges press the seams open to reduce bulk (fig. 8, page 25).

On a curved checkerboard, the seam between it and the next circle is not a curve, but made up of small straight lines, making the wedge construction easier (fig. 9, page 25).

Flying Geese: Press the seams away from the large triangle (fig. 10, page 25).

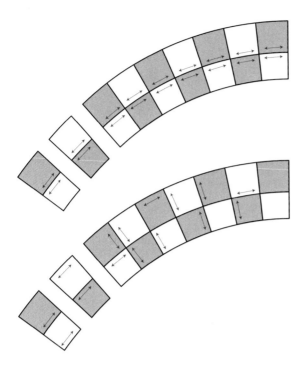

FIG. 8. Checkerboard sections with the grain line marked correctly (top) and incorrectly (bottom)

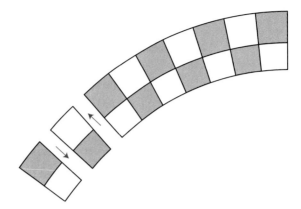

FIG. 9. Seams are straight lines for wedge construction

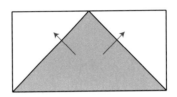

FIG. 10. Pressing diagram for Flying Geese

Faux Geese: These pieces look similar to a row of Flying Geese, but there is a space between the geese. Join the two small triangles and press the seam towards the darker fabric. Add the large triangle and press the seam toward this large triangle. When making rows of Faux Geese I generally press the seams between the geese open (fig. 11).

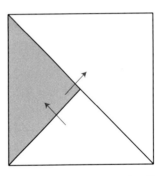

FIG. 11. Pressing diagram for Faux Geese

Triangle-in-a-Triangle: As with the checkerboard design you will need to be consistent with your grain line markings. Start sewing by matching the top and bottom triangles along the marked edges. Press the seam towards the top triangle. Add the side triangles, pressing all seams away from the center (fig. 12).

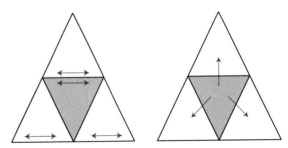

FIG. 12. Grain line markings and pressing directions for Triangle-in-a-Triangle unit

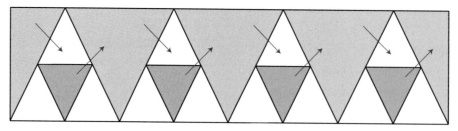

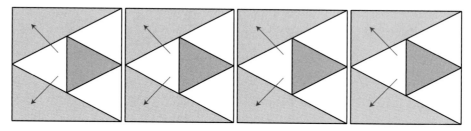

Fig. 13. Pressing directions for Triangle-in-a-Triangle units alternating with plain triangles

Fig. 14. Pressing directions for Triangle-in-a-Triangle with Wings units

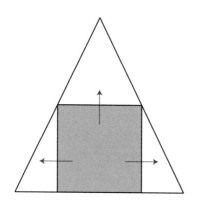

Fig. 15. Pressing directions for House units

Triangle-in-a-Triangle alternating with a plain triangle: It is tempting to press all the seams between these units toward the plain triangle, but this creates unwanted bulk at the point of the triangle. There are two good alternatives (fig. 13). Press all the seams in the same direction or press them open.

Triangle-in-a-Triangle with Wings: Make the Triangle-in-a-Triangle unit first. Add the wings and press the seams toward the wings. If you are making a row of these units it is best to press the joining seams open (fig. 14).

Houses (or Square-in-a-Triangle): Add the side triangles to the square and press the seams away from the square. Add the top triangle and press the seam toward the triangle (fig. 15).

Pressing

There is not always a perfect answer to the question, "Which direction should I press the seam allowances?" Pressing seams to one side can often mean that you will be able to mesh the seams when pinning the next step in the construction process. Pressing seams open can reduce bulk and result in a flatter quilt top but can make matching future intersections more difficult. If you want to do some of your quilting in the ditch, pressing seams to one side will create the ditch needed. If you press the seams open you will not have a ditch to quilt in. Neither of these choices is right or wrong. Each is a legitimate choice and useful for different reasons.

As you progress through the piecing process you will continually need to make choices about how to press the seams. There is never just one way to do things and sometimes you need to experiment with the possibilities to see what works best in any one situation.

As you continue to add pieces, you may want to check to be sure the piecing is accurate and will fit properly when added to another section. A pressing template can be used for this purpose. Trace the outline of a larger section from the master drawing onto a piece of freezer paper or muslin. Add a ¼" seam allowance around this drawn section. Align the pieced unit with the pressing template to check for accuracy. You can iron a freezer-paper ironing template to the ironing board and place the pieced fabric section over it to check for size. You can iron the template to the underside of the sewn section, but be careful when removing it so you do not shred the seam allowances.

If you choose to make the ironing template out of muslin you can iron the sewn section over the template to check for size.

Eventually a pieced section will get large enough so that the stiffness of the freezer paper makes it difficult to maneuver. When this happens you can stop and remove some of the papers. Any paper that has been sewn around on all sides can be removed. Try to leave paper on all the outside edges of each unit as they will be needed for accurately matching the next piece to be added.

Working with Circles and Curves

When copying your design onto freezer paper, extend the divisions of the pieced arcs and circles into the adjacent plain bands. When you are sewing the rings to each other these registration marks will give you visual clues about how the pieces fit together (fig. 16).

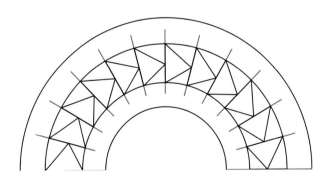

FIG. 16. The extended dividing lines act as reference marks for reassembling the pieced rings.

FIG. 17. Adding colored lines across the drawing will also help with aligning the pieced rings.

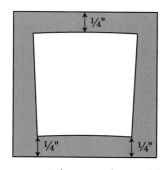

FIG. 18. Use a straight cut when adding seam allowance to small pieces.

seams pressed open

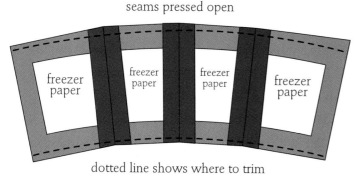

dotted line shows where to trim

FIG. 19. Gently trim the seam allowance on the small curved pieces after they have been joined (as indicated by the dotted line).

Use one or two colored pencils to draw lines across the entire circle. These lines do not need to go through the center of the circle. The colored lines will help position the rings properly when joining them (fig. 17).

Be consistent when you mark the grain line on the pieces in the pieced arcs. Many of the pieces are small enough so that all the edges of the piece look similar and it can be difficult to know which two edges to sew together. Keeping the grain-line marks in the same position on all the pieces can help make it easier for you to know which edges are supposed to be sewn together. (See fig. 8 on page 25.)

When you are cutting out the fabric and adding the ¼" seam allowance to a small curved edge it is faster and more accurate to start by treating the curved edge as a straight edge. For an outer curve, trim the edge with the ¼" mark on your ruler at the center of the curve. For an inner curve align the ¼" mark with the points at both ends of the curve (fig. 18).

After the ring has been pieced you can go back and gently trim the curved edge. It will create a smoother edge and will make attaching the rings to each other an easier task. On an outside curve you will be trimming a bit of fabric at the seam line. On an inside curve you will be trimming a bit of fabric at the center of the curve between the seam lines (fig. 19).

On longer curved edges it would waste too much fabric to use the same straight-line trimming method. For these pieces it is better to trim the ¼" seam allowance by eye. If you doubt your ability to accurately trim by eye, use a small ruler to mark a series of dots ¼" from the edge. You can then connect the dots and trim the seam along the marked line.

The plain rings or arcs are generally divided into 4 or 8 segments. You can certainly cut them as entire circles without any seam lines if you wish. I find it easier to handle them as shorter arcs and cutting them this way uses less fabric.

When joining the arcs or circles it is easier to sew these seams with the inside (concave) curve on the top and the outside (convex) curve underneath. The concave curve is quite flexible and the convex curve is more stable. Putting the stable piece on the bottom allows you to have more control of the flexible, unstable concave curve on the top where you can see it and be sure it behaves (fig. 20).

As you add each curved section you will need to remove the freezer paper from the concave edge so it is easier to manipulate. Before taking off the paper you need to carefully mark the inner edge of the curve. Use a washable marker or a light touch with any marker that cannot be easily removed. Use the edge of the freezer paper to mark the seam line and transfer any registration marks onto the seam allowance. Then remove the freezer paper.

It seems most logical to start at the center of the design and add the rings or arcs until you reach the outside edge. This creates a problem. If you mark the inner edge and remove the freezer paper from ring 1 you can sew ring 1 to the center. But when you go to the next step and are ready to add ring 2 to the outer edge of ring 1 the freezer paper has already been removed from ring 1 and you no longer have your beautifully stable edge.

The solution is to start at the outer edge of the design. Mark the inner edge of the largest ring or frame, remove its freezer paper, and add that ring to the next smaller ring. When that seam has been completed, mark the inner edge, remove the freezer paper, and add this inner edge to the next smaller ring. Continue this process until you add the combined rings to the center circle. Sewing the rings in this order allows you to retain the stabilized convex edge and use it to your advantage.

After you have transferred the reference markings, traced the seam line, and removed the freezer paper, it is time to pin the rings together. Match the colored reference points first. Pin about every 4–5 inches between these points matching the marked lines from the division of the pieced arcs to the actual pieced seam lines. Pinning every 4–5 inches is sufficient and you will be able to easily fit the top curve onto the stable bottom one. Sew a smooth curve from pin to pin keeping the edge of the top curve matched to the edge of the bottom curve.

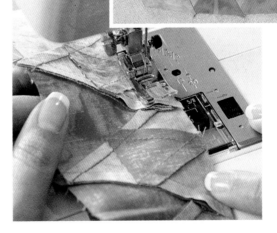

FIG. 20.

About the Projects

By their very nature these designs do not fit easily into the usual square and half-square triangle formulas that we generally use to figure yardage for our quilts. Yardage estimates *are* given for each project, but these are just estimates. It is necessary to have adequate fabric so you have plenty of room to place the freezer-paper templates correctly based on their grain line and to allow for space between the pieces so they can be cut apart with the ¼" seam allowance added. Pieces with long thin points require a surprisingly large amount of fabric when the seam allowance is added. Be aware that the fabric estimates are only guidelines and you may need to adjust the amounts that are listed.

The companion CD has full-size patterns from which you can trace your freezer-paper patterns. They are formatted for printing at home or printing professionally.

The Print at Home patterns are tiled to print on 8½" x 11" paper. Use a light box to align the registration marks (-⊕-) and tape the pages together. The Print Professionally patterns are formatted to print on 36" wide paper, available at commercial copier and blueprint companies. Five of the patterns will print on a single sheet. The four largest patterns will print in two or three sections. Overlap the sections to align them.

Some of the project patterns are completely numbered for you and in others the numbering is left for you to complete. In some of the patterns it is easier to number just one section at a time and start over with #1 as you work on a second section.

Pressing suggestions are given when I think it may be important or useful for you to have that information. You may decide to choose a different pressing direction from what is suggested. If you want a ditch for later quilting or open seams for a flatter appearance you may find it better to make your own decisions about the direction in which the seams should be pressed.

Grain line is marked on most patterns. It has been omitted in some and you may make your own choices. Do try to be consistent and stick to one placement choice as you mark the grain line. Keeping the grain line consistent from one section and one shape to another looks better in the final quilt and makes it easier to do the piecing.

NEW DIRECTIONS, detail. Full quilt on page 47.

ACCIDENTAL STARS

QUILT SIZE: 30" x 30"

Some accidents have a happy ending. Four partial stars that were originally meant for the corner sections of another quilt and a single star made as a demonstration of the freezer-paper template procedure were all hanging at the side of my design wall. After seeing them there for many days it occurred to me that they could be combined into one small wallhanging. A happy accident indeed.

The master pattern (on the CD) includes the numbers, grain line, and fabric choices.

Fabrics & Yardage
Black (background): 1 yard
Red: ⅛ yard
Orange: ¼ yard
Yellow: ⅛ yard
Dark green: ¼ yard
Teal: ¼ yard
Mint: ⅛ yard

Construction Steps

1 The center star is pieced exactly like the TRURO STAR (pages 14–19) (figs. 1 and 2, page 34).

ACCIDENTAL STARS, made by the author

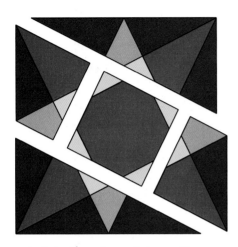

FIG 1. Join the pieces into sections.

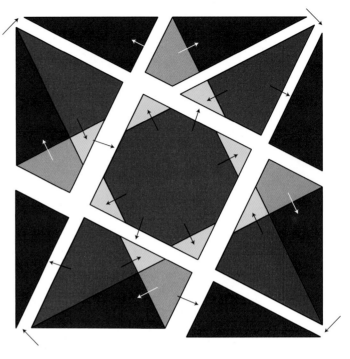

FIG 2. The arrows denote seam pressing directions.

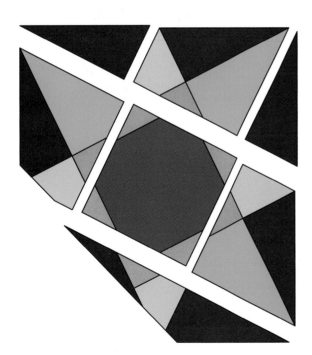

FIG. 3. Make 4.

2 The 4 corners are partial versions of the same basic Truro Star and are pieced in the same manner (fig. 3).

3 The partial stars are joined to the central star (fig. 4, page 35) with Y-seams (page 24).

4 Cut the side borders to measure 5½" x 20½" and add to the quilt. Cut the top and bottom borders to measure 5½" x 30½" and add to the quilt.

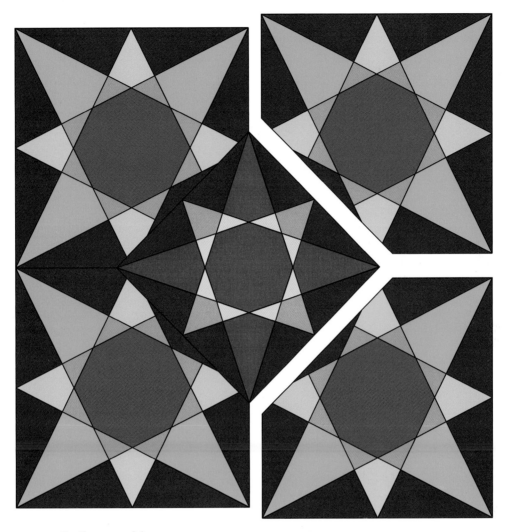

FIG 4. Quilt assembly

SIMPLY CIRCLES

QUILT SIZE: 30" x 30"

SIMPLY CIRCLES, made by the author

When I was asked to demonstrate this freezer-paper piecing technique on HGTV's *Simply Quilts,* they asked me to show how to make my PESWARA quilt in three segments of approximately 5 minutes each! I managed to convince the producer that this was impossible, but offered to show the technique with this design that echoes part of PESWARA.

Notes: *The colors in the checkerboard ring are random. The colors in the Flying Geese ring are organized. There are 24 "geese" in 6 different colors, with 4 different fabrics of each color. The colors progress around the ring in order: blue, yellow, aqua, red, green, orange.*

The master pattern includes numbers and grain line. The background areas are marked with the letter B.

Fabrics and Yardage

Black (background): ½ yard for outer corners and a variety of blacks to total about ½ yard for the remainder of the quilt

Brights: a variety of fabrics in at least 6 color families to total about ¾ of a yard

Multicolor: one 10" x 10" square for the center

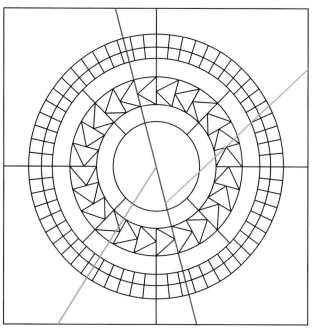

FIG. 1. Adding colored lines across the drawing will help with aligning the pieced rings.

FIG. 2. Flying Geese ring

Construction Steps

1 Draw colored reference lines across the freezer-paper circles to help to properly align the rings when joining them together. Remember that the "circle" between the 2 rows of squares in the checkerboard ring is not an actual circle, but made up of small straight lines (fig. 1).

2 Piece the Flying Geese ring (fig. 2). Press the seams between the geese open or to one side.

3 Piece the checkerboard ring. Press the seam in each wedge toward the black fabric. Press the seams between the wedges open (fig. 3, page 39).

4 Join the arcs to complete each of the plain rings and the 4 corner pieces to form the quilt frame (fig. 4, page 39).

5 Join the rings starting at the outer edge of the design and working toward the center. Mark the inner edge of each ring with the seam line and any reference marks before removing the freezer paper (fig. 5, page 39).

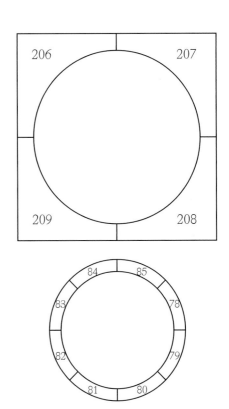

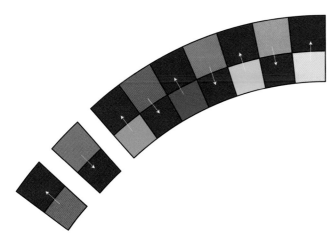

FIG. 3. Checkerboard ring

FIG. 4. Plain rings and frame

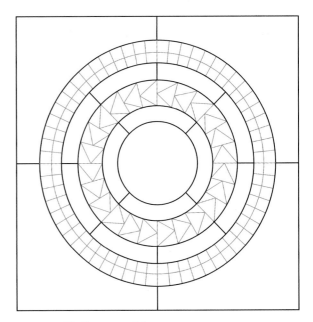

FIG. 5. Quilt assembly

ALISON'S QUILT

My friend Alison D'Bue lives in Cornwall and introduced me to Truro Cathedral. When I decided to tackle the designs from the cathedral floors I started with this design and used it to test the idea of using freezer-paper templates as a piecing aid. The original wallhanging resides in Cornwall with Alison. Kathy McCulloch tested the pattern and sewed a new sample of the quilt.

Notes: In the original version the plain bands were cut as a single piece of fabric. You may choose to divide them into smaller pieces, as shown with dotted lines in the master drawing. If you divide these rings, label the pieces 2a, 2b, 2c, etc.

QUILT SIZE: 32" x 32"

ALISON'S QUILT, made by Kathleen McCulloch, Tucson, Arizona

ALISON'S QUILT, made by the author
COLLECTION OF ALISON D'BUE

The inspiration for ALISON'S QUILT

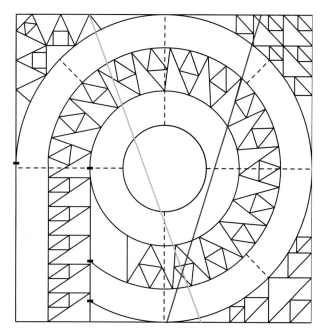

FIG. 1. Adding colored lines across the drawing will also help with aligning the pieced rings.

The long thin points at the outer edge of the quilt can be difficult to draw and to piece. Adding an extra ¼" or so to your freezer-paper drawing will make it easier to draw and piece these very thin points.

The master pattern includes numbers and grain line. Fabric choices are marked for everything except the background. Use background fabric for any unmarked pieces.

Fabrics and Yardage

Light (background): 1½ yards
Light rose: ¼ yard
Rose: ⅜ yard
Grey: ½ yard
Gold: ⅜ yard
Navy: ⅜ yard

Construction Steps

1 Add colored reference lines across the pattern (fig. 1).

2 Piece the curved section. These are Triangle-in-a-Triangle units (page 25) that alternate with larger plain triangles to form a wedge. Leave the marked edge open for now (fig. 2).

Leave this edge open.

wedge   triangle-in-a-triangle

FIG. 2. Leave the seam marked in red open.

3 Piece the 3 corner sections using the diagrams as a guide (figs. 3a–c, page 43).

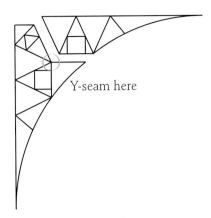
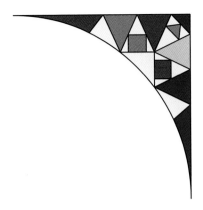

Y-seam here

FIG. 3A. Upper right corner

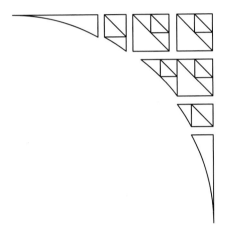
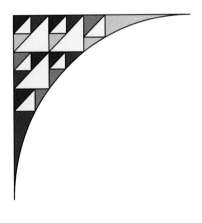

FIG. 3B. Upper left corner

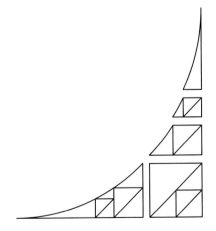
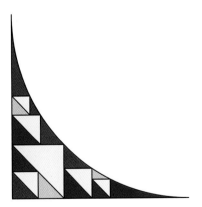

FIG. 3C. Lower left corner

FIG. 4.

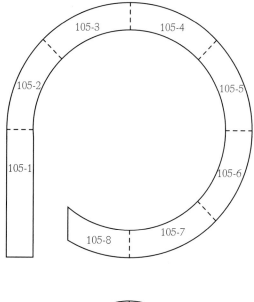

105-3 105-4
105-2 105-5
105-1 105-6
105-8 105-7

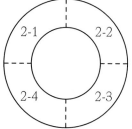

2-1 2-2
2-4 2-3

FIG. 5.

4 Join the 3 corner sections and the long curved triangles (piece #106) to form the outer band (fig. 4).

5 Join the arcs for the 2 plain bands (fig. 5).

6 Join the outer frame, the large plain band, and the pieced band, starting at the outer frame and leaving the straight edge open as marked (fig. 6, page 45).

7 Close the straight edge seam. Backstitch ¼" inch from the inner point so there is a tiny flap at this point. The flap can be folded out of the way when adding the next circle so no raw edge gets caught in the seam (fig. 7, page 45).

8 Add the inner plain band and then the center.

9 Trim off the excess fabric at the outer edges of the quilt if you extended the drawing to make the piecing easier.

10 This quilt does not have a binding and can be finished with an envelope closure or a facing.

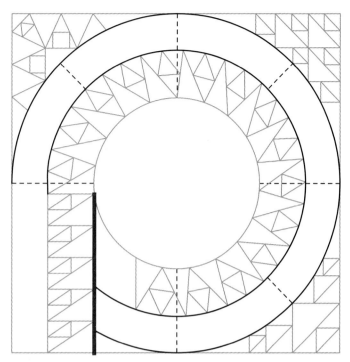

Fig. 6. Leave marked edge open.

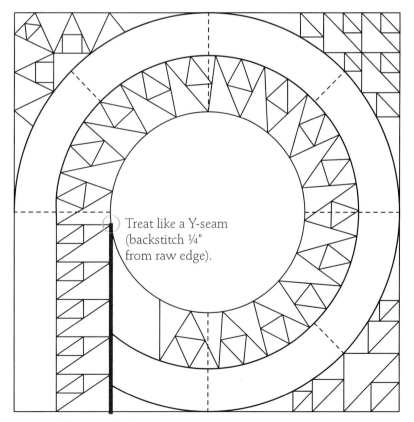

Treat like a Y-seam (backstitch ¼" from raw edge).

Fig. 7. Sew marked seam.

NEW DIRECTIONS

QUILT SIZE: 30" x 30"

W hen The Quilter's Market quilt shop opened in Tucson, the first thing I noticed was the Mariner's Compass mosaic on the floor of the entryway. It seemed obvious that I needed to make a matching wall-hanging for owner Lynda Luiten. The construction is a bit different from the basic freezer-paper method. It includes strip piecing and using the freezer paper on the top of the fabric instead of the back of the fabric.

Notes: *The numbers have been omitted on the master pattern and you can number as you wish. Grain line is included as are most of the fabric choices. Any unlabeled pieces are background.*

The labels for color placement on this design are not reversed. If you prefer to follow the standard freezer-paper method you will need to reverse the color designations in the compass points.

Because we are using strip piecing, we will be ironing the freezer paper to the right side of the fabric. Otherwise, pressing and removing the paper from the underside could shred the seam allowances. The paper will be hidden when you are sewing the seams and you will not be able to use the edge of the paper as your sewing guide. Instead, use your regular quarter-inch marking as a guide and listen for the whisper of the needle grazing the paper as you sew.

NEW DIRECTIONS, made by the author
COLLECTION OF LYNDA LUITEN

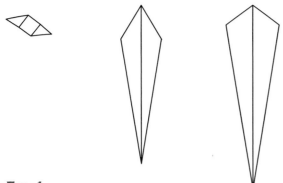

Fig. 1.

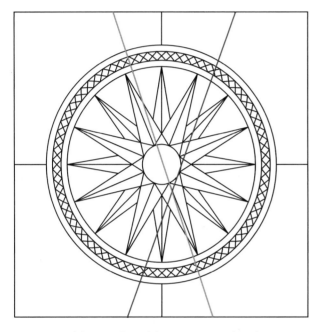

Fig. 2. Adding colored lines across the drawing will also help with aligning the pieced rings.

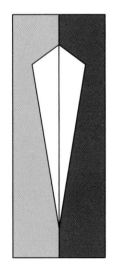

Fig. 3.

Fabrics and Yardage:

Background: 1¼ yards
Brown: ½ yard
Dull gold (or dark beige): ⅓ yard
Green: ⅓ yard

Construction Steps

The compass points and diamond band pieces are cut from strip-sets. Do NOT cut the line down the center of the compass points and do not cut apart the individual pieces in the diamond bands (fig. 1).

1 Draw colored reference lines across the freezer-paper pattern (fig. 2).

2 Cut strips for the compass points.

 4 strips 2¼" gold
 2 strips 2¼" green
 2 strips 2¼" brown

Make 2 strip-sets each of gold & brown strips and gold & green strips. Press the seams open.

3 Iron the longer compass point pattern pieces to the right side of the gold & brown strip-sets and the shorter compass point pattern pieces to the right side of the gold & green strip-sets, aligning the dividing line with the seam. Cut out with a ¼" seam allowance (fig. 3).

FIG. 4. Arrows show the direction to press seams in the wedge.

4 Add the inner curved triangle piece to the 8 longer compass points. Construct 8 wedges with the shorter compass points, pressing the seams as shown (fig. 4).

5 Join the wedges to form the compass (fig. 4).

6 Add the center circle. You may find that it is easier to appliqué this circle than to sew the tight curve. Either method is okay.

7 Cut strips for the diamond banding.

    3 strips 1⅛" green
    6 strips 1½" background

Make 3 strip-sets as shown and press the seams open. Cut the three-piece units from the diamond band pattern and iron onto the front of the strip-sets, aligning the lines on the pattern pieces with the seams. They will not fit exactly since the green sections are not exact squares. You will need to fudge a bit and place the pieces as accurately as possible on the pieced strip (fig. 5).

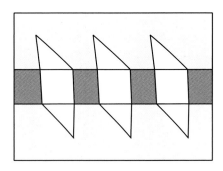

FIG. 5. Make 3 strip-sets.

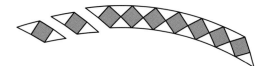

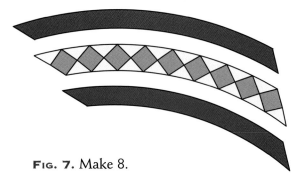

Fig. 6. Make 8.

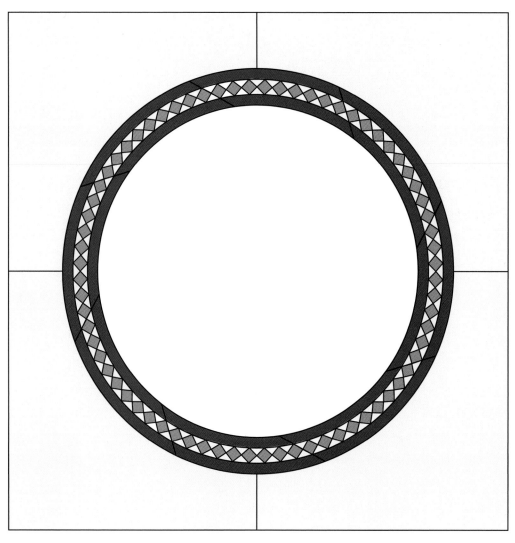

Fig. 7. Make 8.

8 Join the three-piece units into arcs (fig. 6). There are 9 units in each of the 8 arcs. Keep the units in order. Do not try to interchange pieces. They may not fit properly if you mix them up. Press the seams open.

9 Add brown bands to the pieced arcs (fig. 7).

10 Join the brown-edged diamond bands to make a ring (fig. 8).

Fig. 8.

11 Add the background frame to the diamond ring (fig. 8).

12 Add the background/diamond band to the pieced compass (fig. 9).

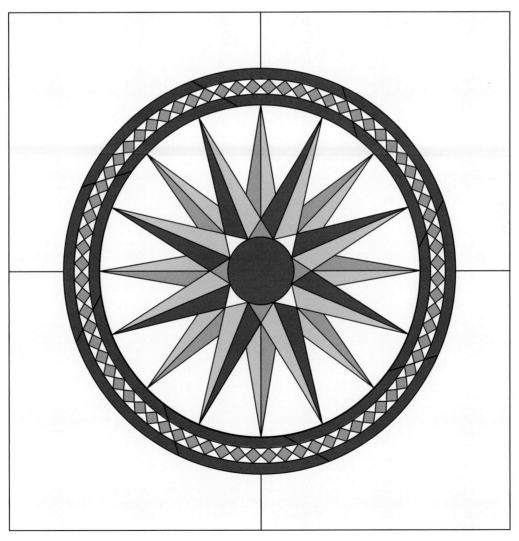

FIG. 9.

CAMPANILE

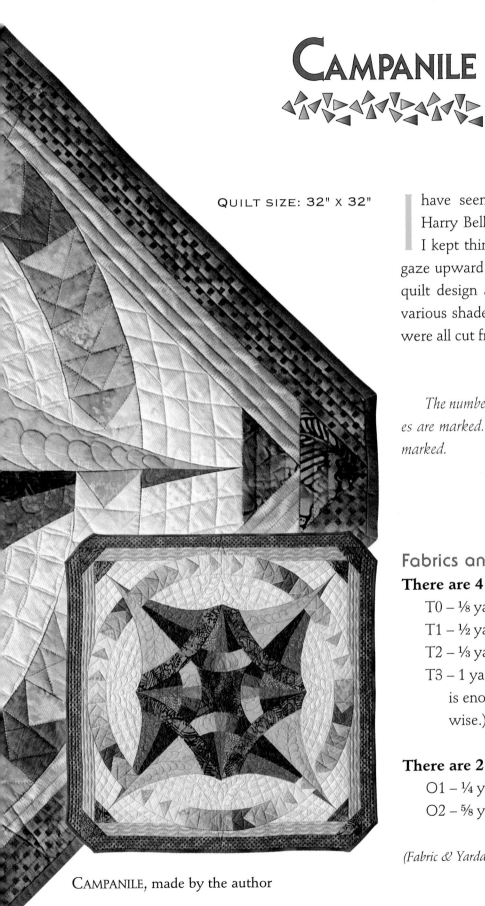

QUILT SIZE: 32" x 32"

I have seen many photographs of the Bell Harry Bell Tower of Canterbury Cathedral. I kept thinking that the shapes seen as you gaze upward into a tower would make a good quilt design and CAMPANILE is the result. The various shades of green in the Faux Geese ring were all cut from one ombre or gradated fabric.

The numbering is left for you to do. The fabric choices are marked. Some but not all of the grain lines are marked.

Fabrics and Yardage

There are 4 shades of beige or tan:

  T0 – ⅛ yard

  T1 – ½ yard

  T2 – ⅓ yard

  T3 – 1 yard for lengthwise border (⅓ yard is enough if you cut the borders crosswise.)

There are 2 shades of orange:

  O1 – ¼ yard

  O2 – ⅝ yard

(Fabric & Yardages continued on page 54)

CAMPANILE, made by the author

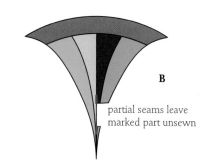

partial seams leave
marked part unsewn

Fig. 1. Make 4 of each pieced section.

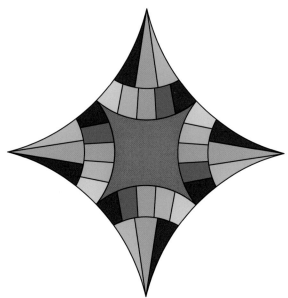

Fig. 2.

(Fabric & Yardages continued)

There are 7 shades of blue:
B1 – ¼ yard
B2 – ¼ yard
B3 – ⅛ yard
B4 – ⅛ yard
B5 – ¼ yard
B6 – ⅛ yard
B7 – ⅜ yard

There are 5 shades of green.
They can be cut from about ¾ yard of ombre fabric, or from ⅛ yard pieces of 5 different fabrics. On the diagram the placement of the darkest and lightest green are noted. Three intermediate shades will be needed between the dark and light values.

In all the colorings the lowest numbered fabric is the lightest and the highest numbered fabric is the darkest.

Construction Steps
The piecing of the individual sections is fairly simple. Joining the sections, especially where the points cross the Faux Geese ring, is a bit more complicated. Those places can be handled with Y-seams (page 24) but I found it easier to use partial seams instead (page 23). Follow the diagrams and take your time with each small part of each seam.

1 Construct 4 of each of the pieced sections A, B, and C (fig. 1, page 54).

2 Join the A sections to the center piece (fig. 2, page 54).

3 Add the B sections. (fig. 3).

4 Join the Faux Geese strips (C) with the lip shapes, then add the corner sections as shown in the diagram. Note the partial seams that will be completed later (fig. 4).

FIG. 3.

5 Add the Faux Geese/lip sections to the center section. The seams are labeled from 1 to 6. Be sure to sew them in this order. The point between seam #1 and #2 (at the top of the lips) is treated like a Y-seam. Sew to within ¼" of the point and backstitch (fig. 5).

FIG. 4. Leave open at marked edges.

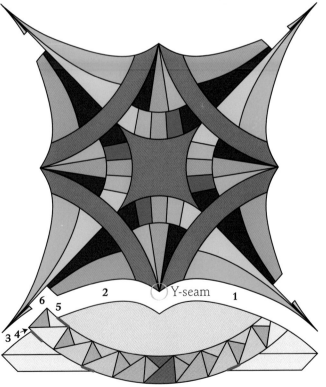

FIG. 5.

6 Once all the lip sections are attached you will still have some partially sewn seams around the edge of the quilt. These will be completed in step 8 (fig. 6).

7 Add the first triangle corners.

8 Add the next border strip to each side. First sew the 2 straight seams, sewing all the way to the raw edge at both ends. Sew the curve including the edges that were previously left open (fig. 7, page 57).

FIG. 6. Red denotes places where the seams are still open. This drawing is *not* a reversed drawing.

9 Add the final triangle corners.

10 Add the final border strips (fig. 7).

FIG. 7.

ABEER'S GIFT

QUILT SIZE: 51" X 51"

Carol Carpenter knew of my love of mosaic designs and showed me a wooden trinket box she had received as a gift, saying she thought I might be interested in using it for a quilt design. My response was that it would make a great quilt design, but that *she* should be the one to make it. With some trepidation—and a promise that I would guide her every step of the way—she agreed to tackle the design. Finding a narrow wavy striped fabric of exactly the right scale and color was a key to translating the trinket box design into a quilt.

Grain line and fabric choices are marked. Numbers are marked on the three main sections, starting over at #1 on each section.

ABEER'S GIFT, made by Carol Carpenter, Tucson, Arizona

Top of trinket box that inspired ABEER'S GIFT

Fabrics and Yardage

Dark purple: 1½ yards
Purple: 1½ yards
Dark blue: ½ yard
Turquoise: ½ yard
White: ½ yard
Light-1: ½ yard
Light-2: ¾ yard
Stripe: 1½ yards

CENTER A. Make 1.

CORNER B. Make 4.

SIDE C. Make 4.

The quilt is constructed in sections. You will make one center (A); 4 corners (B); 4 side sections (C); and 4 border units (D).

Partial seams (page 23) and Y-seams (page 24) are used extensively in this construction. When making your freezer-paper copy, note that the grain line on the striped fabric is marked with more than one straight line. On most fabrics the grain line marking can be placed on either the lengthwise or crosswise grain. These additional lines for the striped pieces remind you to pay attention to the direction of the stripe as you place each pattern piece on the fabric.

The color lavender represents the striped fabric in the figures.

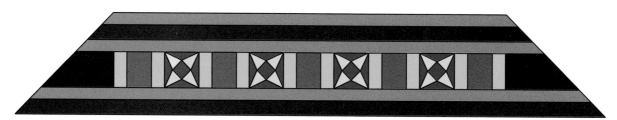

BORDER UNIT D. Make 4.

Construction Steps

SECTION A

1 Make the center 8-pointed star. Be sure to backstitch between the diamonds to leave room for the remaining parts of the Y-seams (fig. 1).

FIG. 1.

2 Add the kite shape between the points of the center star. Treat both ends of these seams as Y-seams, leaving room to add the next pieces (fig. 2).

FIG. 2.

3 Add triangles to one end of the elongated hexagon. Make 8 of these (fig. 3).

FIG. 3. Make 8.

4 Use Y-seams to add a hexagon unit to 4 sides of the central star (fig. 4).

FIG. 4.

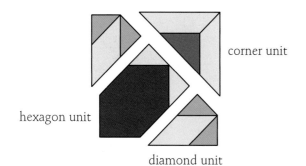

hexagon unit

corner unit

diamond unit

FIG. 5. Make 4.

FIG. 6.

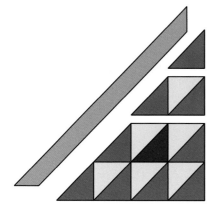

FIG. 7. Make 4.

5 Add triangles to the diamond pieces. Join 2 diamond units to a hexagon unit. Use a Y-seam to make the corner unit. Make 8 corner pieces, saving 4 of them for section C. Add the corner piece to the diamond/hexagon unit. Make 4 of these squares (fig. 5).

6 Use Y-seams to insert the squares into the corners of the central unit (fig. 6).

SECTION B

1 Join half-square triangles into squares, squares into rows, and rows into a large triangle. Add the striped strip to the triangle. Make 4 of these (fig. 7).

2 Sew 4 dark purple strips to frame the turquoise square. Add the striped pieces with a Y-seam. Add the large triangle corners. Make 8 of these—4 will be used for this section and 4 will be used in section C (fig. 8, page 63).

3 Join triangle units from steps 1 & 2 to make 4 squares (fig. 9, page 63).

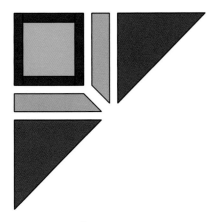

Fig. 8. Make 8.

Fig. 9. Make 4.

Section C

1 Add a striped edge to the remaining 4 triangle units made in step B-2 (fig. 10).

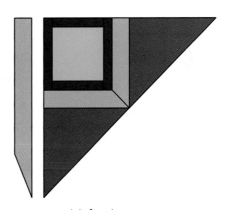

Fig. 10. Make 4.

2 Add the edges to the kite shape. There is a Y-seam at the top and bottom of the kite, but only 2 edges of the seam are sewn now. The marked edge is left open until later (fig. 11).

3 Add a striped edge to the 4 remaining corner units made in step A-5 (fig. 12).

open

Fig. 11. Make 8. Leave with points unsewn for now.

4 Join a corner unit, kite unit, and striped edges following the sewing order as shown in the diagram. Be sure to leave the marked edge of seam #3 open. Make 4 of these units (fig. 13, page 64). Seam #6 will close the bottom of the kite unit.

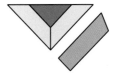

Fig. 12. Corner unit

5 Join the units that make up section C as shown in the diagram. Seam #4 will close the last part of the Y-seam that was left open at the top of the kite. The seam left open at the bottom of the kite on the left is still open (fig. 14).

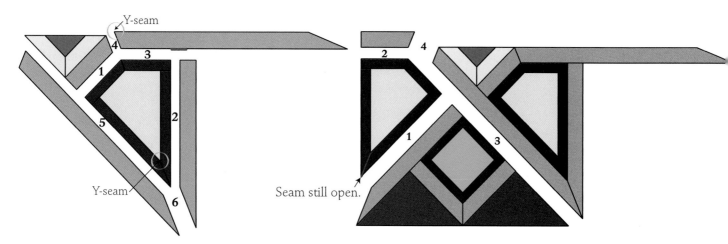

FIG. 13. Make 4. Leave marked edge open. 3 is a partial seam

FIG. 14. Make 4. Close opening at top of kite shape.

JOINING SECTIONS A, B, AND C

1 Join section B to section C. Seam #2 will close the partial seam left open in step C-4. Make 4 of these side/corner units (fig. 15).

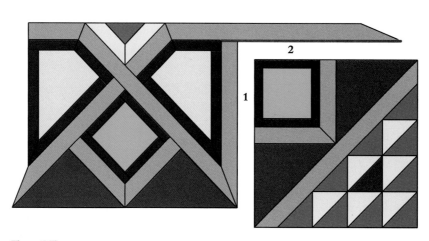

FIG. 15.

2 Add the center to a side/corner unit leaving the marked seam open (fig. 16).

3 Add a second side/corner unit. Sew the long seam first and then the seam that closes the Y-seam from the bottom of the kite to the outer edge (fig. 17).

4 Continue adding the side/corner units until the central square is completed (fig. 18, page 66).

FIG. 16. Leave marked edge open.

FIG. 17.

FIG. 18.

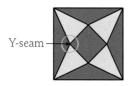

Y-seam

FIG. 19. Make 16.

BORDERS

1 Make 16 stars using Y-seams as shown (fig. 19).

2 Construct the pieced border using the stars, rectangles, and trapezoids.

3 Cut long border strips lengthwise the proper width first, then use your freezer-paper pattern to cut the strips to the proper lengths. The purple borders are cut 1¾" wide. The striped borders are cut 1½" wide. Add the long border strips to the pieced border (fig. 20).

4 Add the borders to the central square, mitering the corners.

FIG. 20. Make 4.

PESWARA

QUILT SIZE: 66" x 66"

PESWARA, made by the author

Four interlocking pieced rings are surrounded by a large circle of Faux Geese. The design started as a copy of a section of the floor of Truro Cathedral but underwent several revisions. Now I doubt if anyone looking at the floor would be able to locate the source of the design.

Notes: The master drawing has not been numbered for you. I recommend that you copy one section at a time onto freezer paper, number just that section, and do the construction. Then repeat for the other sections.

The background fabrics have been marked on the master pattern with the letter B. The remaining fabrics are a random selection of brights.

Fabrics and Yardage

Outer black border: 2 yards will be enough to cut borders lengthwise. The remainder of this fabric can be used for binding and for some of the other black pieces.

Background: many black, dark green, and navy fabrics to total about 4 yards. The only large pieces needed are the curved triangles around the 4 interlocking circles. Each of those pieces uses about ⅓ yard of fabric.

(Fabric & Yardages continued on page 70)

(Fabric & Yardages continued)

Brights: many fabrics to total 3–4 yards

Multicolor: ⅓ yard for the circle centers

Faux Geese: 6 fabrics in graduated values from light to dark. You will need ⅛ yard of the lightest and darkest fabrics and ¼ yard of each of the 4 intermediate fabrics.

The major sections of the quilt are:

1. The 4 interlocking circles—Each circle includes a checkerboard outer band and a pieced inner band. The inner bands are each a different design.

2. The curved triangles that link the 4 circles into one large circle

3. A ring of Faux Geese enclosed by a narrow band of black background fabric

4. Four pieced corners

5. A mitered outer border

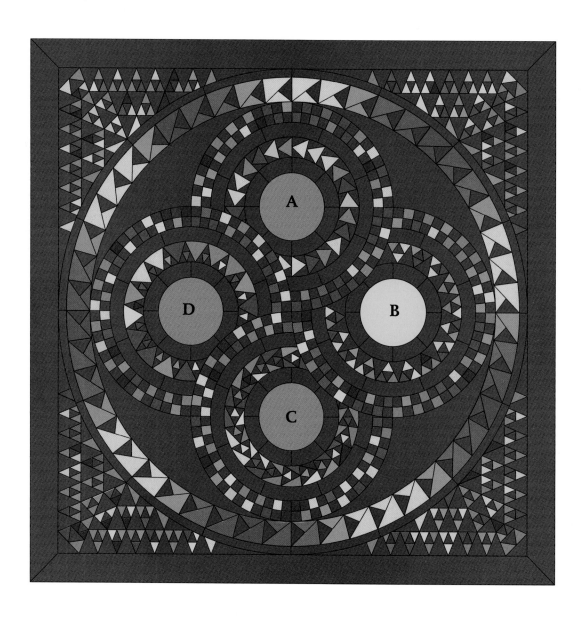

Construction Steps:

1 **Circle A.** Construct the checkerboard ring, the Flying Geese ring, and the plain rings. Join the rings starting at the outer edge and ending in the center (fig. 1).

2 **Circle B.** Construct the checkerboard ring, the Triangle-in-a-Triangle ring, and the plain rings. Join the rings starting at the outer edge and ending in the center (fig. 2).

3 **Circle C.** Construct the checkerboard ring, the Triangle-in-a-Triangle ring, and the plain rings. Join the rings starting at the outer edge and ending in the center (fig. 3).

4 **Circle D.** Construct the checkerboard ring, the Triangle-in-a-Triangle ring, and the plain rings. Join the rings starting at the outer edge and ending in the center (fig. 4).

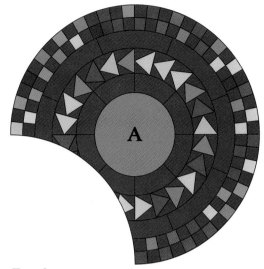

FIG. 1.

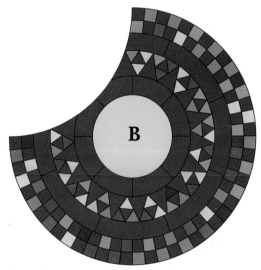

FIG. 2.

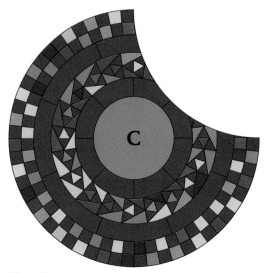

FIG. 3.

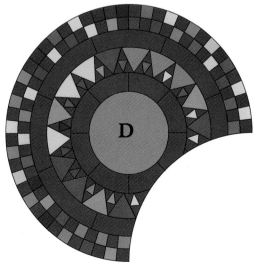

FIG. 4.

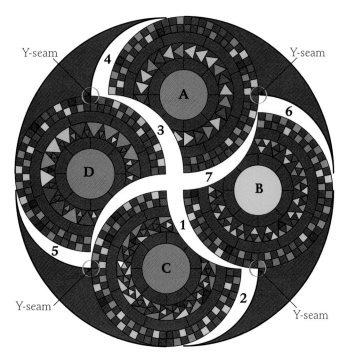

FIG. 5.

FIG. 6.

5 Add a large curved triangle to each of the pieced circles. Treat the inner edge as a Y-seam and backstitch at the point of the paper. Join the circles with their triangle attachments to each other following the 1–7 piecing sequence on the diagram. You will need to remove the freezer paper from the inner edge of the large curved triangle, but try to leave at least some of it on the outer edge to give stability to that edge for further piecing (fig. 5).

6 Piece the Faux Geese ring. The 6 fabrics progress around the circle from light to dark and back again. You will need to omit 2 intermediate steps in the fabric chain somewhere in the progression to make the numbers work out correctly. Add the Faux Geese ring to the center circle. You can remove the papers from the small triangles to give you the flexibility you need, but leave the paper on the large triangle so you still have a stable outer edge (fig. 6).

7 Construct the corner sections following the 1–6 piecing sequence on the diagram. These are rows of Triangle-in-a-Triangle shapes. It looks like there should be Y-seams involved, but it can all be constructed with straight lines (fig. 7, page 73).

8 Join the narrow background bands in groups of 4 and add a corner unit to each group (fig. 8, page 73).

FIG. 7.

FIG. 8.

9 Join the 4 corner units into a large frame and add it to the outer edge of the Faux Geese (fig. 9).

10 Join the frame unit to the center section.

11 Add the outer borders and miter the corners.

FIG. 9.

TRESSA

QUILT SIZE: 42" × 42"

This octagonal design comes from the choir aisle of Truro Cathedral. Some of the construction is done with a more traditional method and the freezer-paper method is employed when the larger pieced sections are joined to each other with the sashing strips. If you carefully compare the pattern to the actual quilt you will find that the pattern calls for 40 Flying Geese in each border but the quilt has only 39 in each border. When I made the quilt I wasn't as careful as I thought I was and the central section was a bit smaller (about half an inch) than planned. I had to choose between making the inner border a bit wider to accommodate 40 Geese or a bit narrower with only 39 Geese. I chose the latter.

Note: Except for the Flying Geese border, the quilt is completely symmetrical. The Flying Geese borders are constructed in groups of 40 geese and can be attached flying either direction, so a reversed drawing is not necessary.

Fabrics and Yardage

10 or more red fabrics to total about 1 yard
12–15 dark fabrics to total about 1 yard
12–15 light fabrics to total 2½ yards
Light inner border ⅓ yard

TRESSA, made by the author

FIG. 1.

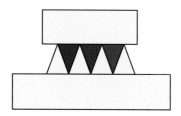

FIG. 2.

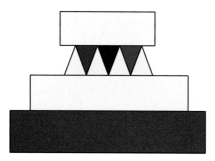

FIG. 3.

The major sections of the quilt are:

1. Octagons
2. Center pieced square with side and corner pieced setting triangles
3. Joining or sashing strips
4. Inner plain border
5. Flying Geese border

Construction Steps

OCTAGONS

1. Make a freezer-paper copy of the pattern but do not cut it apart.

2. Make a new freezer-paper copy of just the triangle sections of one octagon. Cut these apart and piece them using the basic freezer-paper method. Press the seams open (fig. 1).

3. Cut strips of light fabric 2" wide. Add a light strip to the top and bottom of the triangle units. These strips need to be longer than the units (about 6½" for the bottom strip of a full unit and 3" for a half unit). Sew with the triangle unit on top so you can see the thread intersections. This will help you sew perfect points. Press the seams away from the pieced triangles (fig. 2).

4. Cut strips of red fabric 2½" wide and add to the bottom of each unit from step 3. The strip needs to be at least 8" long (4" for the half units). Press the seam toward the red fabric (fig. 3).

Note: *Use the same red fabric for each half unit and its matching reversed half unit.*

5 Cut 1¼" x 6" pieces of beige fabric. Sew these strips between the matching half-units (fig. 4).

6 Cut out an octagon unit from the large freezer-paper drawing and cut it into the sections shown in the diagram (fig. 5).

7 Iron the freezer-paper pattern pieces to the right side of the sewn fabric units, matching lines on the freezer paper to the seam lines of the sewn unit. Trim the fabric ¼" larger than the paper and leave the paper in place (fig. 6).

8 Iron the center octagon paper to the front of a medium-dark or dark grey fabric and trim, adding the ¼" seam allowance. Attach the wedges to the center using Y-seam construction (page 24). When joining the wedges, pin and match all previous seam lines (fig. 7).

9 Repeat these steps to construct the remaining 3 large octagon units.

CENTER SQUARE, SIDE, AND CORNER SETTING TRIANGLES

These sections all share the same pieced band of squares and triangles. It is easiest to piece these in the traditional manner.

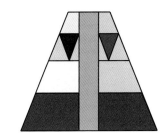

FIG. 4.

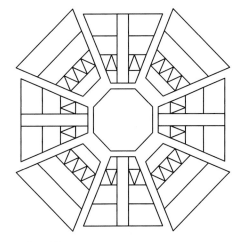

FIG. 5.

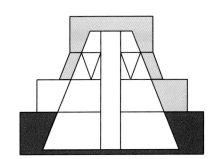

FIG. 6.

FIG. 7.

FIG. 8.

FIG. 9.

partial seam
leave open

FIG. 10A. Center block

FIG. 10B. Side setting triangle

1 Cut 48 light squares 1¼" x 1¼". Cut 8 light squares 2¼" x 2¼". Cut each twice on the diagonal to yield 32 triangles. Cut 32 dark squares 2¼" x 2¼". Cut each twice on the diagonal to yield 128 dark triangles.

2 Join two dark triangles to a light square and press the seams toward the triangles. Make 48 of these wedges. Join a dark triangle to a light triangle to make a larger triangle. Press the seam towards the dark triangle. Make 32 of these units (fig. 8).

3 Join the wedges and larger triangles to make 16 pieced bands (fig. 9).

4 The squares, rectangles, and triangles needed to complete the center square and the setting triangles can be cut with the freezer-paper method. Trace the pattern onto freezer paper, cut out the pieces, iron the pattern pieces to the fabric, and add the ¼" seam as you trim the fabric. You may choose to measure the pieces and cut them in a more traditional manner. Both methods work well. Piece the center and setting triangles as shown in the diagrams (figs. 10a–c).

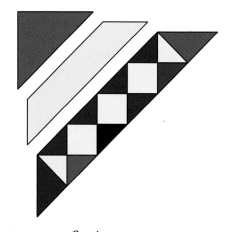

FIG. 10c. Setting corner

SASHING

1 Copy the sashing pieces onto freezer paper. Be sure to label the pieces themselves and on the master copy. Some pieces look nearly alike and you will need to be able to lay them out correctly when you are ready to sew them to the pieced sections. Cut apart, iron them to light fabrics, and trim.

2 Lay out all the pieced sections and the sashing pieces. All of the seams are Y-seams. Do them one at a time in any order that you wish (fig. 11).

INNER PLAIN BORDER

The pieced section should measure 35¾" x 35¾" from raw edge to raw edge. If not, adjust the width of the inner border strips so after they are added, the top will measure 38½" x 38½".

1 Cut your inner border strips 1⅞" x 39¾". Trim the ends of the border strips at a 45-degree angle. Attach the border strips to the quilt top and miter the corners.

FIG. 11. Sashing

FLYING GEESE BORDER

1 Cut 160 rectangles 1½" by 2½" from light fabrics for the geese and 320 squares 1½" x 1½" from dark fabrics for the wings.

2 Draw a diagonal line on the wrong side of the squares. Align a square with the end of the rectangle and sew on the line. Fold the corner of the square out and press. Unfold the corner and trim away the excess. Repeat for the other wing. Make 160.

3 Join the Flying Geese in four rows of 40 geese each. Press the seams between the geese open.

4 Add the first row of geese to the quilt with a partial seam. Add the remaining rows and finish by closing the partial seam (fig. 12).

FIG. 12. Flying Geese border

LOOKING HIGH & LOW

Patterns found in both floors and ceilings of historic buildings are combined to create an entirely new design. A ceiling in Seville, Spain; a floor in Tivoli, Italy; a ceiling in Laon, France; and a floor in Windsor Castle, England, all provided inspiration for this quilt. Although the center motif looks like Celtic appliqué, it is actually machine pieced using the freezer-paper template method.

I started by piecing the ring of linked circles. I knew this would be the hardest part of the quilt to make. I figured if I couldn't successfully accomplish this part I wouldn't have to make the rest of the quilt.

A variety of construction techniques is used in making this quilt. Some sections can be pieced with traditional methods, some with the basic freezer-paper method, and some with other techniques. The yardage amounts given are suggestions only. With a project like this it is always wise to have more fabric than you think you will need. Some of the smallest patches will have more seam allowance than the amount of fabric that shows on the finished quilt and it is easy to underestimate the yardage needed for them. It is also helpful to have enough fabric so you can make choices along the way and change your mind about what fabric is appropriate for each section.

I suggest you read through *all* the instructions for this quilt before starting on any of the construction.

Each section is pieced independently and the sections are then joined together. Let's start by identifying the different parts of the quilt and discussing the fabrics used in each of them. Both the discussion and instructions refer to colors from the original quilt. We'll work from the center out toward the outer edge of the quilt.

The center section is an octagon shape made of red-orange and black fabrics separated by narrow gold lattice. This octagon is framed by light aqua window panes separated by more gold lattice. The center section ends with narrow wedges of dark aqua fabric that turn the octagon into a circle (fig. 1).

FIG. 1.

QUILT SIZE: 81" X 81"

The next section looks like a giant flower with 8 gold petals on an aqua background. It is made in 6 concentric rings of pieced triangles. Each ring is a bit wider than the previous one, giving the design a curved effect. Each ring has pieced outward-facing triangles made of 4 smaller triangles and unpieced inward-facing triangles. In the petal sections, the inward-facing triangles and the centers of the outward facing triangles are yellow. A few of the centers are lime green or fuchsia to add a bit of variety. The fabrics surrounding the tiny yellow centers are orange. In the background sections the large triangles and tiny centers are aqua and the triangles surrounding the tiny centers are gold. This gold is the same fabric used in the window lattices. I used a variety of yellow, orange, and aqua fabrics in this section (fig. 2).

A ring of linked circles surrounds the flower petals. A zigzag ribbon of aqua runs through the circles. You can emphasize the ribbon effect by choosing an aqua fabric with a vertical design on it. Don't try to use a regular stripe as the pieces that make up the ribbon do not have parallel edges. The red circles are made of 5 different shades ranging from dark red to orange. The fabrics are placed so the coloring goes from dark to light and back to dark again, but do not have a regular pattern. One color progression is shown on the master drawing with color A being the lightest fabric and color E being the darkest. The rings are edged with a narrow rim of black on both the inner and outer edges (fig. 3).

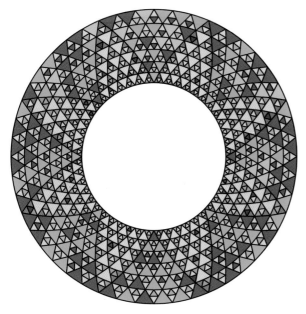

FIG. 2.

FIG. 3.

OPPOSITE: LOOKING HIGH & LOW, made by the author

FIG. 4.

The center, flower petals, and linked circles rest on a floor of geometric tiles interrupted by large black curved triangles. The on-point squares at the tile intersections are all from one yellow fabric. The tiles are constructed in 4 rows with 4 shades of red-orange, ranging from dark to light (fig. 4).

The final section of the quilt is another window pane section with aqua window panes and gold lattice. The binding is the same gold fabric as the lattice, giving the appearance of a slightly wider outer frame for the windows (fig. 5).

FIG. 5.

Fabrics and Yardage:

Yellow: ¼ yard each of 5 different yellows for the flower petal section (1¼ yards total) ½ yard for the small squares in the tile section

Gold: 3½ yards for the window lattices, flower petal section, and binding

Orange: 1 yard total of a variety of oranges for the flower petal section

Reds & oranges: 1 yard of each of 5 different fabrics, shading from dark red to orange (5 yards total) for the linked circles and tile floor

Light aqua: ¼ yard for the inner window panes

Aqua: 2¼ yards for the outer window panes 1 yard for the ribbon in the linked circle section 1¾ yards total of a variety of aquas for the flower petal section and edging of the central section (use one fabric for the edging)

Black: 2½ yards

Lime-green & fuchsia: scraps

Construction:

Center Section: Use the basic freezer-paper piecing method to construct this section. Make 4 kite shapes (fig. 6) and 4 reversed kite shapes. Connect the kite shapes with the lattice pieces.

FIG. 6.

Make 8 window sections (fig. 7). Join the window sections to the kite center with Y-seams. Add the narrow curved edges to complete the center circle.

Option: *If you like to appliqué you could cut the red center as one piece and appliqué the lattice strips onto that center. The windows could also be constructed with appliquéd lattice strips.*

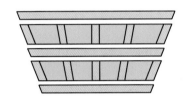

FIG. 7.

Flower Petal Section: You can certainly use the basic freezer-paper method to construct this section, but you will probably get bored very quickly. There are 6 separate rings of pieced triangles and 240 triangles in each ring. That makes 1440 individual pieces of freezer paper if you use the basic method. Because the pieces in each ring are repeated over and over again, I suggest using a slightly different freezer-paper method.

Make one ring at a time, then join them to form the entire flower petal section.

Start by copying one of the Triangle-in-a-Triangle units from the first row onto freezer paper. (It doesn't matter if you start with the smallest row or the row with the largest pieces.) Mark the grain line and fabric choice on each of the 4 triangles before cutting them apart. Iron

FIG. 8.

FIG. 9.

FIG. 10.

FIG. 11.

FIG. 12.

the center triangle pieces to a stack of the correct fabrics and trim the edges ¼" larger than the freezer-paper template. Do the same with the three outer triangles *but* on these add a little more seam allowance at the straight-of-grain edge (fig. 8, page 85).

Sew the outer triangles to the center triangle. Because the outer triangles are a bit too long you don't have to be extremely accurate when adding them but be sure to sew an accurate ¼" seam at the edge of the center triangle (fig. 9).

Make another freezer-paper copy of the Triangle-in-a-Triangle unit. Iron it to the right side of the pieced section, matching the lines of the center triangle to the seam lines (fig. 10).

Trim this section, adding a ¼" seam allowance (fig. 11). For now you can trim the curved line as a straight line, the edge will be trimmed later. You will be able to reuse this one template several times before having to make a new one.

Copy the single large triangle piece onto freezer paper, mark the grain line, and use this template to cut the appropriate triangles. Again, you can cut the curve as a straight line for now (fig. 12).

Make a short ring section, alternating 4 Triangle-in-a-Triangle units with 4 plain triangles (fig. 13, page 87).

Copy a section of the ring this same length onto freezer paper to use as an ironing template. Press the ironing template to the right side of the pieced section, aligning the drawn lines with the seam lines (fig. 14). Leave the freezer paper attached until everything has cooled. This will help the section keep its shape. Trim the curved ¼" seam allowances before removing the freezer paper.

Continue making the sections for this ring, blocking them with the ironing template. Join the sections to complete the ring.

Make all 6 rings, then join them to complete the flower petal section.

Even though you have blocked the pieces as you sewed each group, the final section may not lie completely flat. Copy a larger portion of the design onto freezer paper and use it as an ironing template to flatten everything. Adjust minor imperfections so the flower petal section lies as flat as possible before it is attached to another part of the quilt.

Ring of Circles: Use standard piecing techniques for this section. If you wish to use the freeezer-paper method you will need to reverse the drawing *(trace the rings from the back of the master pattern)*. Be sure to add registration marks when you make your freezer-paper copy from the master drawing. You will use Y-seams to make the centers of the circles (fig. 15).

Add the partial ring to complete each of the 26 rings. When joining the rings to each other, back stitch ¼" from each end of the curved seam as indicated (fig. 16). You will need this small flap of seam allowance when you add the black edgings.

FIG. 13.

FIG. 14.

FIG. 15.

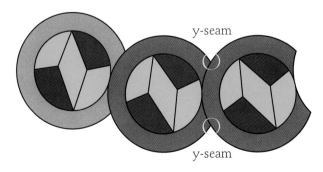

y-seam

y-seam

FIG. 16.

FIG. 17.

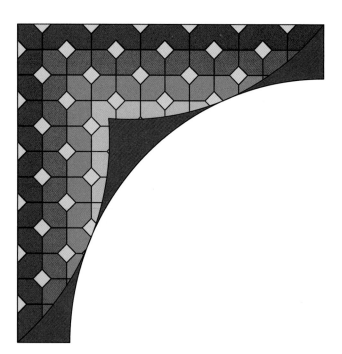

FIG. 18.

Cut the black edgings with freezer-paper templates, adding a bit more than a ¼" seam allowance at the outer edges. This will make the narrowest edge easier to handle. Sew about 3–4 circles together, then add the black edgings to this group. The seams that join the black edgings to the circles are added as curved Y-seams (fig. 17).

Continue adding a few circles and edgings at a time until the entire ring is completed.

Background Tiles: The background tiles can be pieced using templates. There are only two different shapes. Make a template for each shape. The templates can be used multiple times before you will need to make a new one. All of the seams are Y-seams.

At the edges where the large curved triangles fit it looks like there are some odd-shaped pieces. Instead of trying to make these shapes, it is easier to make full sections of the tiles first. Use freezer-paper ironing templates to block sections of the tile pattern as you sew it together (fig. 18). After the sections have been blocked the curved edge can be trimmed ¼" larger than the paper template.

Make freezer-paper patterns for the curved triangles. Join the triangles to the trimmed tile sections with Y-seams.

Outer Window Pane: Use basic freezer-paper piecing for this section. The master pattern shows suggested places for the seams in the lattice of this section (fig. 19). You may decide to make different choices. Be aware that if you want long lattice pieces that travel the entire distance of the outer edge of the quilt you will need to cut these pieces early in the construction process so you have enough fabric length. I chose to seam those long pieces. The original quilt actually has even more seams than those shown on the master drawing simply because I had a limited supply of gold fabric by the time I started on the window section and had to make do with shorter pieces of fabric.

Option: You could choose to cut large sections of aqua fabric and appliqué lattice strips onto the aqua window fabric. You may need more fabric than recommended if you choose this option.

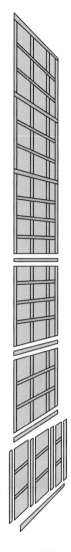

FIG. 19.

QUILT ASSEMBLY. Join the sections as shown.

Gallery

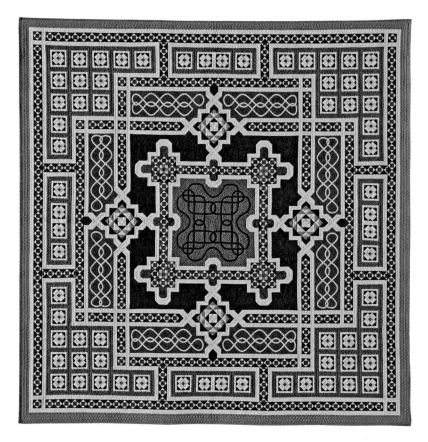

OSGOODE HALL, 67" x 67", made by the author and Jo Cady-Bull, Tucson, Arizona. Osgoode Hall is a heritage building in Toronto, Canada, and is part of the court system and law school. A friend gave me a picture of the floor in the atrium and I used that as the basis for this quilt. In the photo there is a large statue covering the center of the floor. Since I did not know what was under the statue I thought a Celtic appliqué would look nice there. Unfortunately, I do not appliqué. I know how, but choose not to. I asked Jo Cady-Bull if she would like to work on the quilt with me and design the appliqué for the center and one other section of the quilt. She agreed.

Later I saw her working with a Japanese ink and wondered if we could find a way to use it for the 432 three-quarter inch and the 68 half-inch red squares. She figured out a way to use a scrapbooking punch and freezer paper to make those 500 painted squares. That means I did not have to sew 4 triangles to the corners of each of those tiny red squares. Whew! Even so, the quilt contains 4205 pieces of fabric, 20 yards of quarter-inch appliquéd bias, and 500 inked squares. We had a great time working together on this project.

ABOVE: MOSAIC TILE QUILT, 56" x 64", made by Jessica Duke, Tallahassee, Florida. Jessica saw a photograph of the floor in San Vincenzo Abbey, Italy, and wrote to the photographer asking permission to use the photo as the basis for her quilt design. The striped fabric was the perfect choice and was used to great advantage. The floral inner border adds a different feeling to the quilt than it would have with a more expected tone-on-tone fabric.

RIGHT: CAUGHT ON A DREAM, 38" x 38", by Kathryn E. Wald, Tucson, Arizona. The tile design on the Piazza del Campidoglio in Rome inspired Kathryn's quilt. Michelangelo's design on the ground of this historic square is beautifully translated into a quilt pattern. Using short straight lines for the outer circles does not detract from the design and allows the construction to be done without having to sew any curves.

ABOVE: ROMAN HOLIDAY, 82" x 82", made by Sally Gould Wright, Los Angeles, California. Sally used several techniques including appliqué, piecing, and painting. The pictorial motifs are based on Roman ruins in and around Bath, England. Her pieced mosaic circles and compasses beautifully frame the motifs.

LEFT: GEESE GONE WILD, 34" x 34", made by Janet Downing, Tucson, Arizona. Janet's original design features a brightly colored checkerboard center and a border of elongated Flying Geese. She experimented with angles that she may not have attempted without the freezer-paper template method.

About the Author

J ean Biddick is an award-winning quilt-maker, author, and teacher whose special-ty is creating stunning machine-pieced master-pieces. Her thirty years of classroom experience, first as a math teacher and then as a teacher of quilt-ing, has given her the ability to present detailed information in a clear, easy to understand way that encourages success in quilting students.

She loves watching students accomplish more than they thought they could do and en-joys giving them the technical skills they need to turn their visions into quilts. For more than ten years, Jean's passion has been designing quilts inspired by intricate mosaic tile work seen in cathedrals and historic buildings worldwide.

Jean has received numerous accolades for her beautiful machine-pieced mosaic tile quilts, including awards from American Quilter's So-ciety and the International Quilt Festival. Her quilt TRURO MOSAIC II has hung in Truro Ca-thedral where visitors could see both the tile floor and the quilt it inspired. She is the author of *Blended Quilt Backgrounds,* also published by AQS.

You can learn more about Jean on her Web site, www.jeanbiddick.com.

Photo by Freeze Frame Fotography

MORE CARROTS, PLEASE, 16" x 16", made by the author. At some point I wondered if it would be possible to make a miniature version of a tile floor quilt. I used designs from my PESWARA quilt as the basis for this quilt. The pieces were so small that I had to alter the basic piecing method. I used strip piecing where possible and worked with groups of pieces at a time. I also cut strings of the pattern and instead of cutting the pieces completely apart I used a press-and-fold method from the top side of the fabric. Testing different methods and solving problems as they arose al-lowed me to complete this very small and intri-cate design. IN THE PERMANENT OH, WOW! COLLECTION OF THE NATIONAL QUILT MUSEUM, PADUCAH, KENTUCKY.

other AQS books

For today's quilter...
inspiration and creativity from

AQS
Publishing